Laura Rasco! Laura Rowen

God Bless

the USA!!!

Melessa Halling

Jonathan Fuge

Proud to be an American

American are good

Jenny Brown

Matt W

Andrew Denning

The
PROMISE
of
AMERICA

Edited by James L. Murat

*Illustrated by Allan Thomas
and Walt Boscamp*

THE MAKEPEACE COLONY PRESS
A DIVISION OF THE MAKEPEACE COLONY, INC.
STEVENS POINT, WISCONSIN

Copyright © 1970
By The Makepeace Colony, Incorporated
Printed in the United States of America
SBN 87741-008-9

ACKNOWLEDGMENTS

The editors of THE MAKEPEACE COLONY PRESS deeply appreciate the kind and generous cooperation and interest of the authors and publishers whose permission to include the poetry and prose selected for our little anthologies has made it possible for us to publish this treasury of the worthwhile in remembrance literature.

We have spared no effort to ascertain the ownership of all copyrighted material as well as the authorship of all material, and to secure permission and make full acknowledgement for such use. If we have unintentionally and inadvertently erred in any respect, we express our sincere regrets and will gladly make any necessary corrections and additions in future printings.

Thanks are due to all authors and publishers whose works are included, among whom are the following:

The theme of this book is the quotation entitled *The Promise of America* on page 7. This quotation is from page 508 of the book entitled YOU CAN'T GO HOME AGAIN by Thomas Wolfe, Harper & Row, 1940, and it is reprinted by permission of Harper & Row, publishers . . . "IF" — FOR GIRLS by J. P. McEvoy reprinted with permission of Mrs. J. P. McEvoy . . .

THE PROMISE OF AMERICA

IF from *Rewards & Fairies* by Rudyard Kipling, copyright, 1910, by Rudyard Kipling, reprinted by permission of Mrs. George Bambridge and Doubleday & Company, Inc. . . . BE STRONG from *This Is My Father's World* by Maltbie D. Babcock reprinted by permission of Charles Scribner's Sons (1901) . . . THE WINDS OF FATE by Ella Wheeler Wilcox reprinted by permission of Rand McNally & Company, publishers, successors to W. B. Conkey Company . . . ABRAHAM LINCOLN 1809-1865 from *A Book of Americans* by Rosemary and Stephen Vincent Benet. Holt, Rinehart and Winston, Inc., copyright, 1933, by Rosemary and Stephen Vincent Benet, copyright renewed, 1961, by Rosemary Carr Benet, reprinted by permission of Brandt & Brandt . . . DO YOU FEAR THE WIND by Hamlin Garland reprinted by permission of Constance Garland Doyle and Isabelle Garland Lord.

To Jim

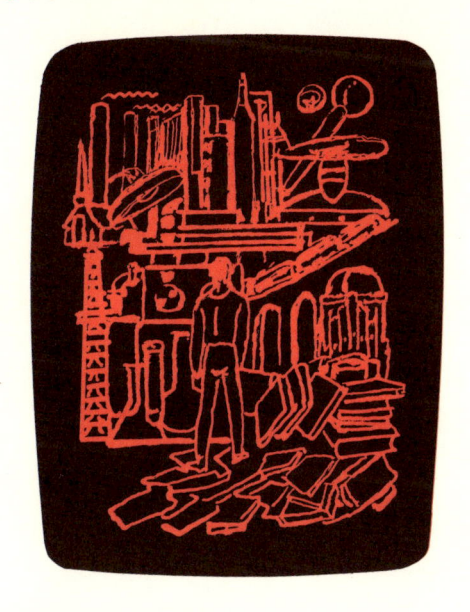

THE PROMISE OF AMERICA

So, then, to every man his chance —
To every man, regardless of his birth,
His shining, golden opportunity —
To every man the right to live,
To work, to be himself, and to become
Whatever thing his manhood and his
    vision can combine to make him —
This, seeker, is the promise of America.

THOMAS WOLFE

YOUR NAME

You got it from your father
It was all he had to give
So it's yours to use and cherish
For as long as you may live.
If you lose the watch he gave you,
It can always be replaced
But a black mark on your name, Son,
Can never be erased.
It was clean the day you took it
And a worthy name to bear
When he got it from his father,
There was no dishonor there.
So make sure you guard it wisely,
After all is said and done
You'll be glad the name is spotless
When you give it to your son.

> A promise made
> Is a debt unpaid.
>
> **ANONYMOUS**

Well done is better than well said.

BENJAMIN FRANKLIN

THE WISDOM OF MY MOTHER

Take time to work —
  It is the price of success.

Take time to think —
  It is the source of power.

Take time to play —
  It is the secret of perpetual youth.

Take time to read —
  It is the fountain of wisdom.

Take time to be friendly —
  It is the road to happiness.

Take time to dream —
  It is hitching your wagon to a star.

Take time to love and to be loved —
  It is the privilege of the gods.

Take time to look around —
  It is too short a day to be selfish.

Take time to laugh —
  It is the music of the soul.

OLD ENGLISH PRAYER

"IF" FOR GIRLS

If you can hear the whispering about you
And never yield to deal in whispers, too;
If you can bravely smile when loved ones doubt you,
And never doubt, in turn, what loved ones do,
If you can keep a sweet and gentle spirit
In spite of fame or fortune, rank or place,
And though you win your goal or only near it,
Can win with poise or lose with equal grace;

If you can meet with unbelief, believing,
And hallow in your heart a simple creed,
If you can meet Deception, undeceiving,
And learn to look to God for all you need;
If you can be what girls should be to mothers:
Chums in joy and comrades in distress,
And be unto others as you'd have the others
Be unto you — no more and yet no less;

If you can keep within your heart the power
To say the firm, unconquerable "No";
If you can brave a present shadowed hour,
Rather than yield to build a future woe;
If you can love, yet not let loving master,
But keep yourself within your own self's clasp,
And not let Dreaming lead you to disaster,
Nor Pity's fascination loose your grasp;

If you can lock your heart on confidences,
Nor ever needlessly in turn confide;
If you can put behind you all pretenses
Of mock humility or foolish pride;
If you can keep the simple, homely virtue
Of walking right with God — then have no fear
That anything in all the world can hurt you.—
And — which is more — you'll be a woman, dear.

J. P. MCEVOY

THE TEEN-AGE COMMANDMENTS

Stop and think before you drink.
Don't let your parents down.
>They brought you up.

Be humble enough to obey.
>You will be giving orders yourself someday.

At the first moment turn away from unclean thinking.
Don't show off when driving.
>If you want to race, go to Indianapolis.

Choose a date who would make a good mate.
Go to church faithfully. The Creator gives us a week.
>Give Him back at least an hour.

Choose your companions carefully. You are what they are.
Avoid following the crowd. Be an engine, not a caboose.
Recall the original Ten Commandments.

THE MADISON (WIS.) CAPITAL TIMES

EVEN THIS SHALL PASS AWAY

Once in Persia reigned a King
Who upon his signet ring
'Graved a maxim true and wise,
Which, if held before the eyes,
Gave him counsel at a glance,
Fit for every change and chance.
Solemn words, and these are they:
"Even this shall pass away."

Trains of camels through the sand
Brought his gems from Samarcand;
Fleets of galleys through the seas
Brought him pearls to match with these.
But he counted not his gain
Treasures of the mine or main;
"What is wealth?" the king would say;
"Even this shall pass away."

In the revels of his court
At the zenith of the sport,
When the palms of all his guests
Burned with clapping at his jests;
He amid his figs and wine,
Cried: "Oh loving friends of mine!
Pleasure comes but not to stay;
Even this shall pass away."

Fighting on a furious field,
Once a javelin pierced his shield;
Soldiers with a loud lament
Bore him bleeding to his tent;
Groaning from his tortured side,
"Pain is hard to bear," he cried,
"But with patience, day by day, —
Even this shall pass away."

Towering in the public square,
Twenty cubits in the air,
Rose his statue, carved in stone.
Then, the king, disguised, unknown,
Stood before his sculptured name
Musing meekly, "What is fame?
Fame is but a slow decay—
Even this shall pass away."

Struck with palsy, sere and old,
Waiting at the gates of gold,
Said he with his dying breath;
"Life is done, but what is death?"
Then, in answer to the King,
Fell a sunbeam on his ring.
Showing by a heavenly ray,
"Even this shall pass away."

      THEODORE TILTON

CHARITY

There is so much good in the worst of us,
And so much bad in the best of us,
That it ill behooves any of us
To find fault with the rest of us.

IF—

This classic selection by the great British writer, Rudyard Kipling, has been a great favorite of monologists for many years. We invite you to refer to the delightful companion piece "If—For Girls" by J. P. McEvoy on page 10.

If you can keep your head when all about you
   Are losing theirs and blaming it on you;
If you can trust yourself when all men doubt you,
   But make allowance for their doubting too;
If you can wait and not be tired by waiting,
   Or, being lied about, don't deal in lies,
Or, being hated, don't give way to hating,
   And yet don't look too good, nor talk too wise;

If you can dream—and not make dreams your master;
   If you can think—and not make thoughts your aim;

If you can meet with triumph and disaster
  And treat those two impostors just the same;
If you can bear to hear the truth you've spoken
  Twisted by knaves to make a trap for fools,
Or watch the things you gave your life to broken,
  And stoop and build 'em up with wornout tools;

If you can make one heap of all your winnings
  And risk it on one turn of pitch-and-toss,
And lose, and start again at your beginnings
  And never breathe a word about your loss;
If you can force your heart and nerve and sinew
  To serve your turn long after they are gone,
And so hold on when there is nothing in you

Except the Will which says to them:
"Hold on";
If you can talk with crowds and keep
your virtue,
Or walk with kings—nor lose the common touch;
If neither foes nor loving friends can
hurt you;
If all men count with you, but none
too much;
If you can fill the unforgiving minute
With sixty seconds' worth of distance
run—
Yours is the Earth and everything that's
in it,
And—which is more—you'll be a Man,
my son!

RUDYARD KIPLING

POLONIUS' ADVICE TO HIS SON

This above all; to thine own self be true;
And it must follow, as the night the day,
Thou canst not then be false to any man.

From Hamlet
WILLIAM SHAKESPEARE

A THING OF BEAUTY

A thing of beauty is a joy for ever;
Its loveliness increases; it will never
Pass into nothingness; but still will keep
A bower quiet for us, and a sleep
Full of sweet dreams, and health, and
    quiet breathing.

JOHN KEATS

A WORD AND A SMILE

Don't hurry through life with a frown on your face,

And never a moment to spare

For the word and the smile are always worth while

In a world full of trouble and care.

There are others with burdens as heavy as yours,

Hearts weary with aching and pain,

That are longing to hear just a word of good cheer,

Will you let them be pleading in vain?

Don't feel that misfortune has singled you out

And made you her own special prey,

For you may be sure there's no home so secure

But that trouble will enter some way.

UNKNOWN

BE STRONG

Be strong!
We are not here to play, to dream, to drift;
We have hard work to do, and loads to lift;
Shun not the struggle — face it; 'tis God's gift.

Be strong!
Say not, "The days are evil. Who's to blame?"
And fold the hands and acquiesce — oh shame!
Stand up, speak out, and bravely, in God's name.

Be strong!
It matters not how deep intrenched the wrong,
How hard the battle goes, the day how long;
Faint not — fight on! Tomorrow comes the song.

MALTBIE DAVENPORT BABCOCK

GIFTS TO GIVE

To a personal enemy, forgiveness;
To a friend, your heart;
To your child, a good example;
To your father, deference;
To your mother, conduct that will make
 her proud of you;
To yourself, respect;
To all men, charity.

ORIGIN UNKNOWN

REMEMBER — The value of time.
The success of perseverance.
The pleasure of working.
The dignity of simplicity.
The worth of character.
The power of kindness.
The influence of example.
The obligation of duty.
The wisdom of economy.
The virtue of patience.
The improvement of talent.
The joy of originating.

BULLETIN

LOOK UP!

Look up! and not down;
Out! and not in;
Forward! and not back;
And lend a hand.

EDWARD EVERETT HALE

One man with courage makes a majority.

ANDREW JACKSON

I NEVER SAW A MOOR

I never saw a moor,
I never saw the sea;
Yet know I how the heather looks,
And what a wave must be.

I never spoke with God,
Nor visited in heaven;
Yet certain am I of the spot
As if the chart were given.

EMILY DICKINSON

THE WINDS OF FATE

One ship drives east and another
    drives west,
With the self-same winds that blow,
  'Tis the set of the sails
  And not the gales
That tell them the way to go.

Like the winds of the sea are the
    winds of fate,
As we voyage along through life,
  'Tis the set of the soul
  That decides its goal
And not the calm or the strife.

              ELLA WHEELER WILCOX

THE WORLD NEEDS MEN

The world needs men:
... who cannot be bought.
... whose word is their bond.
... who put character above wealth.
... who possess opinions and a will.
... who are larger than their vocations.
... who do not hesitate to take chances.
... who will not lose their individuality in a crowd.
... who will be as honest in small things as in great things.
... who will make no compromise with wrong.
... whose ambitions are not confined to their own selfish desires.
... who will not say they do it "because everybody else does it."
... who are true to their friends through good report and evil report, in adversity as well as in prosperity.
... who do not believe that shrewdness, cunning and longheadedness are the best qualities for winning success.
... who are not shamed or afraid to stand

for the truth when it is unpopular, who can say "no" with emphasis, although all the rest of the world says "yes."

SUPERVISION MAGAZINE

MAKE FRIENDS

He who has a thousand friends has not
   a friend to spare,
And he who has one enemy shall meet
   him everywhere.

ALI BEN ABU TALEB

A RULE

   Do all the good you can,
   By all the means you can,
   In all the ways you can,
   In all the places you can,
   At all the times you can,
   To all the people you can,
   As long as ever you can.

JOHN WESLEY

SUCCESS

Success is speaking words of praise,
In cheering other people's ways,
In doing just the best you can,
With every task and every plan,
It's silence when your speech would hurt,
Politeness when your neighbor's curt,
It's deafness when the scandal flows,
And sympathy with others' woes,
It's loyalty when duty calls,
It's courage when disaster falls,
It's patience when the hours are long,
It's found in laughter and in song,
It's in the silent time of prayer,
In happiness and in despair,
In all of life and nothing less,
We find the thing we call success.

ANONYMOUS

This is the final test of a gentleman: his respect for those who can be of no possible service to him.

WILLIAM LYON PHELPS

TRY, TRY AGAIN

'Tis a lesson you should heed,
    Try, Try again;
If at first you don't succeed,
    Try, try again;
Then your courage should appear,
For, if you will persevere,
You will conquer, never fear;
    Try, try again.

T. H. PALMER

You can do as much as you think you can
But you'll never accomplish more;
And if you're afraid of yourself, young
    man,
There's little for you in store.
For failure comes from the inside first,
And it's there, if you only knew it,
But you can win, though you tackle the
    worst,
If you feel that you're going to do it!

DR. FRANK CRANE

IT SHOWS IN YOUR FACE

You don't have to tell how you live each day;
You don't have to say if you work or you play;
A tried, true barometer serves in the place,
However you live, it will show in your face.

The false, the deceit that you bear in your heart
Will not stay inside where it first got a start;
For sinew and blood are a thin veil of lace —
What you wear in your heart, you wear in your face.

If your life is unselfish, if for others you live,
For not what you get, but how much you can give;
If you live close to God in His infinite grace —
You don't have to tell it, it shows in your face.

ANONYMOUS

SUCCESS

There's no thrill in easy sailing
  When the skies are clear and blue,
There's no joy in merely doing things
  Which anyone can do,
But there is some satisfaction
  Which is mighty sweet to take,
When you reach a destination
  Which you thought you couldn't make.

ANONYMOUS

JUST BE THE BEST

If you can't be a pine on the top of
 the hill,
Be a shrub in the valley; but be
The best little shrub by the side of
 the rill;
Be a bush if you can't be a tree.

If you can't be a bush, be a blade of
 grass,
And some highway happier make.
If you can't be a muskie, then just
 be a bass,
But the livliest bass in the lake.

We can't all be captains, we've got
 to be crew.
There's something for all of us here.
There's big work to do, and there's
 lesser to do,
And the task we must do is the near.

If you can't be a highway, then just
 be a trail;
If you can't be the sun, be a star.
It isn't by size that we win or we fail —
Be the best of whatever you are!

DOUGLAS MALLOCH

POOR RICHARD'S WISDOM

From a slip of the foot you may soon recover,
But a slip of the tongue you may never get over.

BENJAMIN FRANKLIN

No wind serves him who has no destined port.

MONTAIGNE

My life shall touch a dozen lives before this day is done,
Leave countless marks for good or ill ere sets this evening sun.
My life shall touch a million lives in some way ere I go
From this dear land of struggle to the land I do not know.
So this the wish I always wish, the prayer I always pray:
Let my life help the other lives it passes by this way.

STRICKLAND GILLILAN

THE SIZE OF YOUR HEART

It isn't the size of your house so much
   That matters so much at all
It's the gentle hand and its loving touch,
   That maketh it great or small.
The friends who come and the hour they go,
Who out of your house depart,
Will judge it not by the style you show
   It's all in the size of your heart.

It isn't the size of your head so much,
   It isn't the wealth you found
That will make you happy — it's how you touch
   The lives that are all around.
For making money is not so hard —
   To live life well is an art:
How men love you, how men regard,
   Is all in the size of your heart.

ANONYMOUS

Lord, reform thy world, beginning with me.

PRAYER OF A CHINESE CHRISTIAN

DO YOU FEAR THE WIND

Do you fear the force of the wind
The slash of the rain?
Go face them and fight them,
Be savage again.
Go hungry and cold like the wolf
Go wade like the crane;
The palms of your hands will thicken,
The skin of your cheeks will tan,
You'll grow ragged and weary and
    swarthy
But you'll walk like a man!

HAMLIN GARLAND

A SMILE

Let others cheer the winning man,
There's one I hold worth while;
'Tis he who does the best he can,
Then loses with a smile.
Beaten he is, but not to stay
Down with the rank and file;
That man will win some other day,
Who loses with a smile.

BREATHES THERE THE MAN WITH SOUL SO DEAD

Breathes there the man with soul so dead
Who never to himself hath said,
This is my own, my native land!
Whose heart hath ne'er within him burned,
As home his footsteps he hath turned
From wandering on a foreign strand?
If such there breathe, go, mark him well;
For him no minstrel raptures swell;
High though his titles, proud his name,
Boundless his wealth as wish can claim,
Despite those titles, power, and pelf,
The wretch, concentred all in self,
Living, shall forfeit fair renown,
And, doubly dying, shall go down
To the vile dust from whence he sprung,
Unwept, unhonored, and unsung.

SIR WALTER SCOTT

It is easier to get people to promise to do better tomorrow than it is to get them to do their best today.

I am not bound to win,
But I am bound to be true.
I am not bound to succeed,
But I am bound to live up to what light
    I have.
I must stand with anybody that stands
    right;
Stand with him while he is right,
And part with him when he goes wrong.

ABRAHAM LINCOLN

ABRAHAM LINCOLN 1809-1865

Lincoln was a long man.
He liked out of doors.
He liked the wind blowing
And the talk in country stores.

He liked telling stories,
He liked telling jokes.
"Abe's quite a character,"
Said quite a lot of folks.

Lots of folks in Springfield
Saw him every day,
Walking down the street
In his gaunt, long way.

Shawl around his shoulders,
Letters in his hat.
"That's Abe Lincoln."
They thought no more than that.

Knew that he was honest,
Guessed that he was odd,
Knew he had a cross wife
Though she was a Todd.

Knew he had three little boys
Who liked to shout and play,
Knew he had a lot of debts
It took him years to pay.

Knew his clothes and knew his house.
"That's his office, here.
Blame good lawyer, on the whole,
Though he's sort of queer.

"Sure, he went to Congress, once,
But he didn't stay.
Can't expect us all to be
Smart as Henry Clay.

"Need a man for troubled times?
Well, I guess we do.
Wonder who we'll ever find?
Yes — I wonder who."

That is how they met and talked,
Knowing and unknowing.
Lincoln was the green pine.
Lincoln kept on growing.

          ROSEMARY CARR AND
          STEPHEN VINCENT BENET

THE DAY'S DEMAND

God give us men! A time like this demands
Strong minds, great hearts, true faith and ready hands;
Men whom the lust of office does not kill;
Men whom the spoils of office cannot buy:
Men who possess opinions and a will;
Men who have honor—men who will not lie;
Men who can stand before a demagogue
And damn his treacherous flatteries without winking;
Tall men, sun-crowned, who live above the fog
In public duty and in private thinking;
For while the rabble, with their thumb-worn creeds,
Their large professions and their little deeds,
Mingle in selfish strife, lo! Freedom weeps,
Wrong rules the land, and waiting Justice sleeps.

JOSIAH GILBERT HOLLAND

INSCRIPTION ON THE STATUE OF LIBERTY IN NEW YORK HARBOR

Give me your tired, your poor,
Your huddled masses yearning to breathe free,
The wretched refuse of your teeming shore,
Send these, the homeless, tempest-tossed to me:
I lift my lamp beside the golden door!

THE PRICE OF FREEDOM

These are the times that try men's souls. The summer soldier and the sunshine patriot will, in this crisis, shrink from the service of their country; but he that stands it now, deserves the love and thanks of man and woman. Tyranny, like hell, is not easily conquered; yet we have this consolation with us, that the harder the conflict, the more glorious the triumph. What we obtain too cheap, we esteem too lightly; it is dearness only that gives everything its value. Heaven knows how to put a proper price upon its goods; and it would be strange, indeed, if so celestial an article as FREEDOM should not be highly rated.

THOMAS PAINE

GIVE ME LIBERTY OR GIVE ME DEATH

Gentlemen may cry peace, but there is no peace. The war is actually begun.

The next gale that sweeps from the north will bring to our ears the clash of resounding arms. . . . Is life so dear, or peace so sweet as to be purchased at the price of chains and slavery? Forbid it, Almighty God. I know not what other course others may take. But as for me— Give me liberty, or give me death!

PATRICK HENRY

SECOND INAUGURAL ADDRESS

With malice toward none, with charity for all, with firmness in the right as God gives us to see the right, let us strive on to finish the work we are in, to bind up the nation's wounds, to care for him who shall have borne the battle and for his widow and his orphan, to do all which may achieve and cherish a just and lasting peace among ourselves and with all nations.

ABRAHAM LINCOLN

When Franklin Delano Roosevelt entered the presidency, the country was staggering under a crushing economic depression. His first inaugural address, delivered March 4, 1933, was designed to re-kindle confidence in the hearts of the American people.

THE ONLY THING TO FEAR IS FEAR ITSELF

"This great Nation will endure as it has endured, will revive and will prosper. So, first of all, let me assert my firm belief that the only thing we have to fear is fear itself—nameless, unreasoning, unjustified terror which paralyzes needed efforts to convert retreat into advance."

And later in the same speech, he said:

"Happiness lies not in the mere possession of money; it lies in the joy of achievement, in the thrill of creative effort. The joy and moral simulation of work no longer must be forgotten in the mad chase of evanescent profits. These dark days will be worth all they cost us if they teach us that our true destiny is not to be ministered unto but to minister to ourselves and to our fellow men."

FRANKLIN D. ROOSEVELT

TODAY'S NEEDS

Our crisis today is in reverse.

We find ourselves rich in goods, but ragged in spirit; reaching with magnificent precision for the moon, but falling into raucous discord here on earth.

We are caught in war, wanting peace. We are torn by division, wanting unity. We see around us empty lives wanting fulfillment. We see tasks that need doing, waiting for hands to do them.

To a crisis of the spirit, we need an answer of the spirit.

To find that answer, we need only look within ourselves. . . .

The simple things are the ones most needed today if we are to surmount what divides us, and cement what unites us.

To lower our voices would be a simple thing.

In these difficult years, America has suffered from a fever of words: From inflated rhetoric that promises more than it can possibly deliver; from angry rhetoric that fans discontents into hatreds; from bombastic rhetoric that postures instead of persuading.

We cannot learn from one another until we stop shouting at one another — until we speak quietly enough so that our words can be heard as well as our voices . . .

The lesson of past agony is that without the people we can do nothing; with the people we can do everything . . .

We can build a great cathedral of the spirit — each of us raising it one stone at a time, as he reaches out to his neighbor, helping, caring, doing . . .

Until he has been part of a cause larger than himself, no man is truly whole . . . No man is fully free while his neighbor is not. To go forward at all means to go forward together . . .

RICHARD M. NIXON
from Inaugural Address

WHY NOT?

Some men see things as they are, and say, "Why?" I dream of things that never were, and say, "Why Not?"

ROBERT F. KENNEDY

JOHN F. KENNEDY
INAUGURAL ADDRESS

Let every nation know, whether it wishes us well or ill, that we shall pay any price, bear any burden, meet any hardship, support any friend, oppose any foe, in order to assure the survival and the success of liberty. . . .

And so, my fellow Americans, ask not what your country can do for you; Ask what you can do for your country.

My fellow citizens of the world: Ask not what America will do for you, but what together we can do for the freedom of man.

JOHN F. KENNEDY

The following words were found on a scrap of paper pasted on the inside cover of the New Testament which General Robert E. Lee always carried with him:

Put any burden on me; only sustain me.
Send me anywhere; only go with me.
Sever any tie but this which binds me to Thy service and to Thy heart.

The Makepeace Colony is dedicated to the idea of sharing with you the inspiration, joy and comfort that we have found in the selections contained in this series — to bring you "a treasury of the worthwhile in remembrance literature." We hope you have found our little volumes a pleasure to give, and a delight to receive.

If you have written or found selections which you would like to share with others in future editions of this series, we invite you to forward them to us.

This little volume was designed and illustrated by Allan Thomas and Walt Boscamp. The type is 12 Baskerville, the text paper is substance 70 offset, vellum finish, and the printing is by the two-color offset process, with hard covers and Smyth sewed binding — all designed to make this series of remembrance gift literature of lasting value.

THE MAKEPEACE COLONY PRESS